Syria Is in the
World

Ara Shirinyan

palm
PRESS
2007   Long Beach, CA

Copyright ©2007
First Edition

ISBN
987-0-9789262-0-5
0-9789262-0-X

$15.00

Printed in the U.S.A.

Cover art: Argee Geronca
Book design and typesetting: Karen Sheets

palm
PRESS

Palm Press
143 Ravenna Drive
Long Beach, CA 90803
www.palmpress.org

For my parents, Arshak and Tigranuhi

Contents

Expatriates

This letter
striktly
confidentially!

We recomend to destroy
immediately on reading!

Goverment FR accepted decision
about publications
in the press list
secret employee MBD USSR.

Our organization &

RCSDPF
(Russian Christian
Social Democratic Party
of Fairness),

against everydey optinion
that folk must know thein
own squaler

Well if folk is aware of
then, but here with must
not suffer inncent people
a children, relatives, friends.

Your mother long years
was a secret informer
MBD Armenia,
at following years
MBD Russia.

On our hands
file is found
with her personal deal.

In this file
her personal statement
written with the own hands

about desire to help organ
of the deals,

photographies of the diffe¬rent years,
recepts about reception of the money
remunerations and certain¬ly official reports

on thein own friends,
familiar own
colleague.
Many from her victims
at present
live in USA.

Considering your public position,
presense of the strong family,
rewiews compatriot about you,
we consider undesirable appearanse
of the name of your mother
in these list.

If our information to you indifferent ignore her.

But if information you interest,
find member RCSDPF,
which will agree to be a
go-between between you and our
organization. There is no need to

denote him in
essense of the deal.

He will sent you file in sealed envelope,
He possible to sey that this trouble on
adjusting deal about emigrations.

Our caution is dictated life.

When we have sent such letter
Gevork Terzian he was
voiced approximately so,
that i
abore that
my Fater was an
informer KGB!

You is called up in two weeks.

In these days on telephone voiced
answer must only you.

You will name password — ULOD.

You then and there send
number,
which you will give
chosen by you mem¬ber
RCSDPF.

IT! is a situation

Playact nomadic
CIA tow
Bet nephew
O to phone niftily
Linocut Kilo the event
Chords conman
Beat cupfuls
O to phone
Hot monocot
Key ash
Key heir
BE caper
Kook toppled howl
A bow to Key
At meat flapped eat
Bicep
Me Corpse

POEM for a new RUSSIA

M0M amply   Tonic-Cubes-
Machine mobs took notebook:
Fall-Bluffed Loans Excelled

Bikini eyeful flesh
Corny flab partakes
Bypath prep
: -
Roof   calf
HUM   TO
Broke   cape-
Knee hole:

Common
Pylons nab nap-
Packed, prance-

Helm Crumbs accept Coma, prism Keg, lamp Chug,
Condone fleered biker.
Amps lucked
Hack Macho, Economy
Ammo crank   school   Haunt-

Bloom: Likeably LUKE-fax
Used Sax nearby Hair:
Poacher car cabana incises mite yap-

Pie — rasp
Namibia Sea
Mbeki pox
Karate Ham
Potpie norm
Hoe Flay
Each fled

Ox-nape
Hobo Throb Cabbie
In Tamper-
Phobic iambs

Elf of Moby
Kin tub
Pylon neck
Mono pearled

Bleak new Cocky chaos

    "Ha" imbibed Moscow squared
    Storm crowds
    Scattered by land

Soviet Poets

The optimistic, resolute rhythms of his poetry of the 1930s gave way to heroic solemnity in the pre-war and war years. It speaks to us across the ages about love, loyalty, patriotism, and hope.

Her poetry throbs like a taut wire, and her choice of words is usually of a conversational variety.

His emotional and intellectual poetry is analytical in character. A highly cultured man, he has the acumen of a critic and the intuition of a pedagogue.

His melodious poetry is intuitive and spontaneous in character, and his rhythms are vigorous, clear-cut, and ingenious.

Her graceful, plastic poetry responds with great subtlety of feeling to people's happiness, suffering, and hopes. Her verse is like exquisite filigree work, its intricate patterns and modulations reflecting the subtlest shades of feeling and mood, sometimes as light as a fleeting sigh.

Her writing is not flamboyant, her words and images are simple, and she leaves a great deal unsaid but merely hinted at. Spiritual phenomena, such as memory, dreams or fantasies, are so perfectly sculptured that they become tangible things.

Her life and art are forever bound up with Leningrad, the cradle of the Revolution. Her tragic verse is an appeal for trust in the people who in painful travail gave birth to the new, just world.

His lyricism is rooted in his native Byelorussia and conveys the inimitable colors of its woods and fields, the clear sparkle of its rivers, and the bustle of its cities. Music has been written to many of his verses.

His openly committed, free verse reflects the changes in the life of his country. His later work shows a more lyrical approach to life and the world around him.

His poetry traces the development of man's sense of civil responsibility.

His poetry is a blend of philosophic symbolism, humor, and a truthful rendering of details taken from life around him.

His poems convey imagery exaggeratedly complicated and startling. The nerve center of his poetry is a feeling of alarm for the insecurity of the world in the atomic age.

His poetry, which takes the form of lyrical meditations, explores with insight and sympathy the fate of the ordinary, inconspicuous man.

The popularity of his poetry is explained by its amazing and quite rare combination of natural talent, the tradition of naïve ancient folk myths and songs, and modern literary culture.

He is seeking his own ways of developing modern poetic diction and in doing so draws on the wealth of the Ukrainian language. He is an innovator not only as regards to form but also as regards to content.

He is especially popular with students and young people. His poetry is imbued with a sense of civic responsibility, it is publicistic in character, and constantly focused on the main problems of the day. He is a consistent and ardent champion of revolutionary ideas and principles.

The main theme of his poetry is Nature and its ties with Man, approached from a philosophical point of view.

Her earlier vision of the world was rather superficial and illustrative but then she began to come into her own as a mature poet tackling serious moral problems of the society around her.

The chief characteristic of the work of this poet, who extols the omnipotence of the intellect, are the virtuosity in his use of words, the ingenuity of his plots, and the chiseled polish of the structure of his poems.

His philosophical poetry treats the essence of eternal human values and concepts. His attitude to life and art is a firmly positive one: he is a genuinely modern poet, a man of courage and integrity.

A master of epic poetry, he follows the tradition of psychological reflection. The style of his lyric verse is vividly metaphorical.

An exceptionally gifted lyric poet, he writes in the aphoristic, austerely reserved manner peculiar to Caucasian folk poetry. He writes of fortitude in the face of tribulation, staunchness of spirit, and on such simple universal themes as love, motherhood, and fidelity to one's duty.

Originally he belonged to the constructivist group of poets and sought to express the wisdom of the revolution in a dry, matter-of-fact manner, using stark, precise formulae. His later work captures the reader's imagination with its wealth of ideas and its emotional force.

He was born into a peasant family and worked at a factory after school. Later, he enrolled at the Literary Institute of Moscow. Some of his many widely read volumes reflect the glory of the people's heroism in the war against Germany.

He is a true virtuoso, a skilled master of language with a sensitive understanding of the secret inner associations of words.

A gifted poet of epic cast, he has also published collections of lyric verse. He tackles a wide range of themes such as the evolution of social concepts, the individual and the community in wartime, the problems of the atomic age, and the individual's psychological make-up.

His poetic gift attained its peak in his "Lyric Notebook," an inspired collection on which he worked for many years. It contains philosophical reflections on life and death, meditations on the value of life and the value of art, and thought about time and eternity.

He is a popular poet and 1962 Lenin Prize winner. Many of his poems are hymns to the powerful intellect of Man, the toiler and fighter who has harassed atomic energy and explored outer space.

He began writing poetry during the war. The harsh realities of war imposed their strong influence on his poetry. His work bears the imprint—more distinctly than does that of his contemporaries—of the tragedy of those who grew up in war.

He is a widely known children's poet and satirical writer. There can hardly be a child in the Soviet Union who does not know his poetry by heart. He has translated "Three Little Pigs" into Russian and many other nursery rhymes and stories for children.

He began by writing poetry about the war and still frequently returns to war themes. The mood of his poetry is highly romantic, and his handling of lofty subjects as remarkably subtle and stirringly profound, without a trace of affectation.

He was a poet of world stature whose genius was complex and contradictory. Son of a well-known painter, he received his philosophical education in Germany. His withdrawal from the trivia of life and the bustle of the surrounding world was an intrinsic part of his nature but his poetry still responded sensitively to all the major, cardinal changes in the world.

He is a well-known bard of the Russian north. He was born and raised in the family of a fisherman. His early poetry is distinguished for its emotional spontaneity, colorful idiom, and revolutionary enthusiasm. Reflections on life make up the content of his most recent poetry, set in the form of lyrical parables.

He is one of our most popular young poets. His style is dramatic and direct. His poetry is composed through the belief that modern poetry should be based on real facts.

He began writing poetry as a schoolboy and published his first book when he was fifteen. His artistic tastes became defined at an early age. His songful lyricism is astutely psychological, his hues are reminiscent of a delicate watercolor, and his picturesque descriptions are vivid and evocative.

He was born in the south of Russia into a poor Jewish family. All know his "Grenada", which was Mayakovsky's favorite poem. It expresses in a most natural way the feeling of international brotherhood which was shared by the people who made the Great October revolution.

He is a gifted poet. In his poetry he has combined the traditions of ancient Armenian, modern Russian, and West-European art. In spite of his great erudition, he does not indulge in Euphuistic intellectualism. On the contrary, his poetry is firmly rooted in real life. He is both an excellent craftsman and a true artist.

He has written many verses about animals, describing their characters, movements, and distinctive traits with competence and not infrequently drawing a paradoxical parallel between these beasts and men.

He is a well-known poet, novelist, playwright, and publicist. He does not write as much poetry nowadays, but in the 1940s he was probably the best loved poet in the Soviet Union. His lyricism is always topical, vividly expressive, and extremely evocative.

He is an original poet who sees the truth of the life around him with a rare clarity and vision. He entered the literary scene when Soviet writers were struggling against the practice of embellishing and varnishing the truth and striving to cultivate a sober, realistic attitude to life.

He devotes all of his poetry to the man of toil, a character faithful in friendship, constant in his affections, undaunted by hardships and capable of taking the rough with the smooth.

The son of a poor peasant, a veteran of the Civil War, an experienced organizer and orator, he entered Russian poetry as a convinced champion of democratic principles in art. He has waged a constant battle with aesthetes and snobs. He despises the exotic romanticism of fantasy, and believes in the harsh truth of reality.

Soviet critics have unanimously acclaimed him for the depth of his historical thinking and for the authenticity with which he portrays the spirit of the ordinary people's life.

He is a poet born of the revolution, a soldier, and traveler. His clear-cut laconic ballads which brought him renown as early as the 1920s sing a hymn to strength and courage inspired by justice.

He is a descendent of Russian Cossacks who emigrated to Asia. The traditions of freedom-loving Cossacks with their cult of physical strength and their enormous vitality find an interesting reflection in his poetry. It is earthy and vivid in imagery, the comparisons are richly sensuous, and the language is colorful and dynamic.

He was born in a mountain village on the Black Sea coast. The image of the road is to be found throughout his work.

He has a distinct identity and a place of his own in Russian poetry as a master of thumbnail stories in verse with a moral to each one of them. His style is aphoristic, and the form he often uses is that of a laconic parable.

His poetry reflects the soul of a man of the 20th century with its torments, impulses, and hope.

In the 1940s his poetry was very colorful in its language, but in subject matter it was superficial and fell short of life's serious demands. However his talent matured, and the last ten or fifteen years have made him one of the best-known of our poets with a deep sense of civic responsibility and a significant message to his readers. He sets high moral standards and demands integrity and an honest attitude to life.

Wheel to Small Flag

the small flags of the east France uses

three equal horizontal bands of green

on yellow color and brands of blue tea

three nets on ones of equal waters

at one with white men

at edges of the white man

rectangle centers them

with crosspiece that connects

all four sides of a small flag

in all four angles, small nets

five appears in themes

with equal horizontal bands

century of black color on gold three equal nets

on yellow black green sharp great intent

star wrap uses popular bread of Africans

the small flag of Bolivia that has covering arms

concentrated in horizontal bands

yellow colors more in width

the white man doubles

and net with three dominates

castle inside center of women

white wraps hang in the vestibule

castles with keys of gold concentrate

in wraps of net with small flags

France used nine equal horizontal lines

blue alternated with white man

blue place inside autumn

meat side most raised

guides behind

rolling woman of white in crosspiece

Greek Orthodoxy

religion established

horizontal bands of country

man of two whites on net

with great record of center

most raised record is net

half is white woman

with rectangle

divided diagonally

in yellows

triangles above low point

green triangles

with orderly molds

small flag concentrates on edge

an advanced part to plow seven colors

five-acute stars

with three nets

most advanced edge that you record

overlapped center of small flag has more

over with symbolic system of mascara

nut in the triangle

of the world Granada

second-largest producer of Indonesia

representation starts

in administrative divisions

small flag of territorial France is used

small flag is blue with pressuring liquid

mold all four sides concentrated with ellipse

directed, vertical ends

contain scene of a beach,

canoes, outriggers, sails

trees, palms, sobriety

Guam states net in bold letters

United States citizen is equal to the vertical band

Blue, free, small

flag tree of a man

covering the arms that concentrate on a woman

white wrap of arm-covering has orderly liquid

Quetzal, national bird, for meet emendation

for sestet vapor September 1821 register

Freedoms, it

originates independence

very cross-section

of pairs and sword frames

white man Saint George proprietor of England

to be equal but smaller line of exercise

flag and finial edge prolong net color and use

popular bread of Africans in Ethiopia

bands of green vertical line

acute with intent

star must blacken wrap of popular African colors

Ethiopia, with isosceles overlapping excess of limit

dove, anger-frames

white man equality rectangle

consent system arms covering small flag tree

aforesaid flag of Australia

the union makes force

beings utilize papal key of white man of acute stars

organized model of women represent members

the old federal republic, center of America

small flag of rescuer will count on emblems

round encircled words

Republic of concentrate

woman wipes small flag of Nicaragua

to leave devices that triangle

encircling word Republic

Nicaragua advances past America in liquid

white woman with stylization

white woman with five petals

flower concentrating on small flag of the United States

guides three bands of equal horizontal lines of saffron

subordinate orange man

will wheel intent

to small flag

WASTE the LAND

O KOPEK, —I eat carp
Groans of Treason in the gulag
Net knows coffins where no
Jury sips—
—RIME
—HEAT
Sandy naiad canoes Hacker,
Ink-tied—
Minted
Baffler odes kin
Blotched Ohhhs
Ohio Paint
A lineage: mere comic navels
Nubs of prey pray

Outfits join bosom of Sunni

Tea in Connecticut
        —Octobers

Seminar-mine harvest
Encore-hornets
Knockout jailing
Hieroglyphs—
—Barbwire cope

Tenor scene limp adopts
Metro opera
Whisper-jibe higher,

Aleppo nonevent
        —NABS bomb

Idioms ask apt

Capture-matted
Dupes
Coke to Barn
Pans nosier flu hymn
Soft to copulate crepe of
　　　—Marred King

Foil-buses
Relic-jug,
Wore—
—Neat mob

Jab borrowed
Antique aura
In scud-adjoined
Exam barrows

Hoo Haas backed with
—Harp
COBRA Chechen
—Choo-choos—
Jihad alibi
Wok anecdotals

In water-tirade:
　　　—Ways jokes hoax
Orally afforded aid
　　　—Woe-oats
Bashful oboe amateur aims at
Twin-imbued eatery
Lettuces,
Beats
These long
Breadlines,
Even-with,
Folk babble
To close-share

Stroll the rubble:
Ruble bubbled

Sea-joints need trousers,
        —Shorts
Bra crane's new sold map
In pie-idled den-militias

Pin-luau
        —Nubs on
        —Spit lips
Inapt
—Loins mix angry

Insulin upon doors: city's flip

Bump-unify uranium slit rims
Noun insipid: gulf's ply business

Housie bid low, buy Fiji
Union jammed with vibraphones
Uzis blossom to quail pups
Opium pinup's huff puff
        —Transactions

Husk-afforded bashful booth
Rows madam's aim: service
        —Gathers food
Deiced hands let go jaw
Debit debt blobs as dew

Hero oafs abort ox, garnish origin
Quota rags dam waves

Junk limo dons argon anchor
Jackals earn ovens

Iterate need to aloe rabbi's inbox
Do reign,
      —Ideate never Harrow
If show hams,
      —Deli violas

Copy and Cope

Culture fleshes through collected repeats of folk tale
The ability to copy makes you cope—the ability to imitate
Each moment of this repeating
Becomes in and another thing

Writings damaged and danger an outside another thing
Transformed such ways that the extracted copy of an influenced
Original—ideas anti to wellbeing,
Vulgar ideas, cultural purity, nation, etc.

Part and power to profits—respiration is representation—one
End of image touches other native folk tradition, pleasing the
    role of
Women, simple juxtaposed things,
Montage tower of the represented

Captured culture cultivated through
Collection word string, touch what you're
Imagined from—balanced body can imitate the ability to
    imitate
Watch the way whole cultures cope so malignly, appearing to
    gather

Toward the presence of information,
We have new for you—the ability
To copy to cope, culture forms land values, ability to river the
Settlement—every moment of this period, let's cope the
    digested

Representation—someone has said
Imitate and imagine the small copper
Penny is able to take you, so
Mimic learn copy and cope

fought and continue to

here's probably televised boy
reports his encounter
pounding olive marginal

these connect to miracles
materialed during hours
shouts from cages definitely case sacred

an established coming to terms
guns graze life stocks
youth-production requires practice chairs
if group does see mobility
mainly, then, there's hope of fraud
family-dosed good thoughts
disgust here of leader legs
by ally-gathering bases
registration specs domestic wellness

the small people-horses
purchase much poor existence;
confidence a large finely eared tomorrow

marvel a calm old occasion
and any-let a good disguest
freely, in order to impatiently marry

afraid-quote

inclined to example the finish of forced kitchens
incident of conscience following without result

that shines of necessity, from horses to the sea
of the victory in the sea, the swelled cheek

be distanced, on exceptionally not she;
done real that makes breathing of governments

assumes dis or taunt can smell the broken place
door glue brought down; possibility obtained from look

like points of fond being coaxed from subject on grid
of the city's great joy, the line-discussed smile,

criminal fence fights, the distant added
decrees in this condition, in individual bread,

blister and drool the edifice in area there selected most
beautiful morning of the participant of union supply,

at the time of window-quotes and required situations, around
excitement, found expired of announced added looks,

next to the feet of society-quote
and considered nose-shout

faction becoming relic

schooldays contribute to
inoperative damaged
nonfunctioning absolute:
the seedbed of nonage minority.
uttermost one-liners. learning to
be cable with more dream.
id wounds bet better on medical.

childhood participates in Brecht ill
or uniformity. in. unrefined liberal male,
photographic device of adolescent
motivation. Becoming youth aged.
news henchwoman mallet
debut nonfiction, always managed
but below-satisfying. arcade bad-town.

part on earth relic becoming faction.
womanhood opera function-fine.
ways bed in form dams syndromed.
schools tribute advertisement.
go overthrow. for thee rest us.
part coming publicity-lute.
morality impact. of. deity diet,
orthodoxy for these yous.

chilled boots sip icebed.
slip on one this civil. something here.
elect, avail, chive.
some period of even life.
become the best possible, termite.
it would be better to methodical.

salute-trench contributes lines.
one more when rigged. or roused.

serpent spends the they like:
we can able become more bad.
self reflex more decording.
then thing.
reap-rise early, to wed one book only.
to know this impact that there's
bad here smell it out clumsy. begin
more ands.

East From Here

Connected by similarities or a common source
The kind of day to regret a sweater

A small area of land used for growing a particular crop, with a
    particular group in mind
All the egos in the same mask

The highest natural male singing voice
Often the problem being not the way a people are but the way they
    are governed

And the business of transporting goods or people
Every time I hear the sound of a siren I would put a comma there

A particular kind or quality of brightness
A building where pigs are kept

A thin pointed stick of wood or plastic used to remove food from
    between the teeth
World produced by well-appointed positions

Feeling or showing sadness because someone has died
Praise a maid in the morning; charge your escape on credit card

Objection to something used to refer to people in general
For hours admiring dry patches in grass

Thing required in order to have success or achieve something
To recall something to mind or become aware of something that
    had been forgotten

Opportunities, like eggs, like travelers without looks
An unplanned and unfortunate event that results in damage, injury,
    or upset of some kind

Produces something as a result, or makes something happen in
a sudden feeling of fear or anxiety, especially among many
people;
The road to ruin and weather in the evening

Giddens' *History of Sneak*

camouflage is very probable to look natural
in some trees and desisted movements of bugs

WWI for the subjective, gratefulness to Freud,
toned down the uniform
its get-up that
chests of many kind
hold many things

also nationalism is birthed
in human beings fast to traction

in plans of ambush they locate Xs on land
they record couplings sometimes through aviation

later, pentagon is portrayed crudely
a medal is arrogantly shaped like a medal

on they

it is the effective nausea insect,
a perpetual country on my back
control recorded ears,
a zoo dealing in policy

living representative integrates,
a representative approach laws days
a latent characteristic lifts directly,
advertises your candidate wells

so: taste leads this investigation semialertly,
do go ahead and nurture cynically
so: kind host the age of egg longs,
a more moral marital tomorrow
so: lineated graph ornate with patriots watches
as you do you

error is obtained and parasitism is small,
questions futile after united
the result assumes the tax is high,
girls to kitchen, boys to factory

find that fact distributes with addition of appearance

again: adult is highly recorded
again: testing ability is semiserious

Flag

three equal vertical bands of black (hoist side), red, and green, with a gold emblem centered on the red band; the emblem features a temple-like structure encircled by a wreath on the left and right and by a bold Islamic inscription above the flag of the UK is used red with a black two-headed eagle in the center two equal vertical bands of green (hoist side) and white; a red, five-pointed star within a red crescent centered over the two-color boundary; the crescent, star, and color green are traditional symbols of Islam (the state religion) blue, with a white triangle edged in red that is based on the outer side and extends to the hoist side; a brown and white American bald eagle flying toward the hoist side is carrying two traditional Samoan symbols of authority, a staff and a war club three equal vertical bands of blue (hoist side), yellow, and red with the national coat of arms centered in the yellow band; the coat of arms features a quartered shield; similar to the flags of Chad and Romania, which do not have a national coat of arms in the center, and the flag of Moldova, which does bear a national emblem two equal horizontal bands of red (top) and black with a centered yellow emblem consisting of a five-pointed star within half a cogwheel crossed by a machete (in the style of a hammer and sickle) blue, with the flag of the UK in the upper hoist-side quadrant and the Anguillan coat of arms centered in the outer half of the flag; the coat of arms depicts three orange dolphins in an interlocking circular design on a white background with blue wavy water below red, with an inverted isosceles triangle based on the top edge of the flag; the triangle contains three horizontal bands of black (top), light blue, and white, with a yellow rising sun in the black band three equal horizontal bands of light blue (top), white, and light blue; centered in the white band is a radiant yellow sun with a human face known as the Sun of May three equal horizontal bands of red (top), blue, and orange blue, with two narrow, horizontal, yellow stripes across the lower portion and a red, four-pointed star outlined in white in the upper hoist-side corner the flag of Australia is used blue with the flag of the UK in the upper hoist-side quadrant and a large seven-pointed star in the lower hoist-side quadrant known as the Commonwealth Star, representing the federation of the colonies of Australia in 1901; the star depicts one point for each of the six original states and one representing all of Australia's internal and external territories; the remaining half is a representation of the Southern Cross constellation in white with one small five-pointed star and four larger, seven-pointed stars three equal horizontal bands of red (top), white, and red three equal horizontal bands of blue (top), red, and green; a crescent and eight-pointed star in white are centered in red band three equal horizontal bands of aquamarine (top), gold, and aquamarine, with a black equilateral triangle based on the hoist side red, the traditional color for flags of Persian Gulf states, with a white serrated band (five white points) on the hoist side; the five points represent the five pillars of Islam the flag of the US is used green with a large red disk slightly to the hoist side of center; the red sun of freedom represents the blood shed to achieve independence; the green field symbolizes the lush countryside, and secondarily, the traditional color of Islam three equal vertical bands of blue (hoist side), gold, and blue with the head of a black trident centered on the gold band; the trident head represents independence and a break with the past (the colonial coat of arms contained a complete trident) the flag of France is used red horizontal band (top) and green horizontal band one-half the width of the red band; a white vertical stripe on the hoist side bears Belarusian national ornamention in red three equal vertical bands of black (hoist side), yellow, and red; the design was based on the flag of France blue with a narrow red stripe along the top and the bottom edges; centered is a large white disk bearing the coat of arms; the coat of arms features a shield flanked by two workers in front of a mahogany tree with the related motto SUB UMBRA FLOREO (I Flourish in the Shade) on a scroll at the bottom, all encircled by a green garland two equal horizontal bands of yellow (top) and red with a vertical green band on the hoist side red, with the flag of the UK in the upper hoist-side quadrant and the Bermudian coat of arms (white and green shield with a red lion holding a scrolled shield showing the sinking of the ship Sea Venture off Bermuda in 1609) centered on the outer half of the flag divided diagonally from the lower hoist side corner; the upper triangle is yellow and the lower triangle is orange; centered along the dividing line is a large black and white dragon facing away from the hoist side three equal horizontal bands of red (top), yellow, and green with the coat of arms centered on the yellow band; similar to the flag of Ghana, which has a large black five-pointed star centered in the yellow band a wide medium blue vertical band on the fly side with a yellow isosceles triangle abutting the band and the top of the flag; the remainder of the flag is medium blue with seven full five-pointed white stars and two half stars top and bottom along the hypotenuse of the triangle light blue with a horizontal white-edged black stripe in the center the flag of Norway is used green with a large yellow diamond in the center bearing a blue celestial globe with 27 white five-pointed stars (one for each state and the Federal District) arranged in the same pattern as the night sky over Brazil; the globe has a white equatorial band with the motto ORDEM E PROGRESSO (Order and Progress) white with six blue wavy horizontal stripes; the flag of the UK is in the upper hoist-side quadrant; the striped section bears a palm tree and yellow crown centered on the outer half of the flag blue, with the flag of the UK in the upper hoist-side quadrant and the Virgin Islander coat of arms centered in the outer half of the flag; the coat of arms depicts a woman flanked on either side by a vertical column of six oil lamps above a scroll bearing the Latin word VIGILATE (Be Watchful) yellow with two diagonal bands of white (top, almost double width) and black starting from the upper hoist side; the national emblem in red is superimposed at the center; the emblem includes a swallow-tailed flag on top of a winged column within an upturned crescent above a scroll and flanked by two upraised hands three equal horizontal bands of white (top), green, and red; the national emblem formerly on the hoist side of the white stripe has been removed—it contained a rampant lion within a wreath of wheat ears below a red five-pointed star and above a ribbon bearing the dates 681 (first Bulgarian state established) and 1944 (liberation from Nazi control) two equal horizontal bands of red (top) and green with a yellow five-pointed star in the center; uses the popular pan-African colors of Ethiopia red with a blue rectangle in the upper hoist-side corner bearing, 14 white five-pointed stars encircling a cogwheel containing a stalk of rice; the 14 stars represent the 7 administrative divisions and 7 states divided by a white diagonal cross into red panels (top and bottom) and green panels (hoist side and outer side) with a white disk superimposed at the center bearing three red six-pointed stars outlined in green arranged in a triangular design (one star above, two stars below) three horizontal bands of blue (top), red (double width), and blue with a white three-towered temple representing Angkor Wat outlined in black in the center of the red band; only national flag to incorporate a building in its design three equal vertical bands of green (hoist side), red, and yellow with a yellow five-pointed star centered in the red band; uses the popular pan-African colors of Ethiopia two vertical bands of red (hoist side and fly side, half width), with white square between them; an 11-pointed red maple leaf is centered in the white square; the official colors of Canada are red and white three horizontal bands of light blue (top, double width), white (with a horizontal red stripe in the middle third), and light blue; a circle of 10 yellow five-pointed stars is centered on the hoist end of the red stripe and extends into the upper and lower blue bands blue, with the flag of the UK in the upper hoist-side quadrant and the Caymanian coat of arms centered on the outer half of the flag; the coat of arms includes a pineapple and turtle above a shield with three stars (representing the three islands) and a scroll at the bottom bearing the motto HE HATH FOUNDED IT UPON THE SEAS four equal horizontal bands of blue (top), white, green, and yellow with a vertical red band in center; there is a yellow five-pointed star on the hoist side of the blue band three equal vertical bands of blue (hoist side), yellow, and red; similar to the flag of Romania; also similar to the flags of Andorra and Moldova, both of which have a national coat of arms centered in the yellow band; design was based on the flag of France two equal horizontal bands of white (top) and red; there is a blue square the same height as the white band at the hoist-side end of the white band; the square bears a white five-pointed star in the center representing a guide to progress and honor; blue symbolizes the sky, white is for the snow-covered Andes, and red stands for the blood spilled to achieve independence; design was influenced by the US flag red with a large yellow five-pointed star and four smaller yellow five-pointed stars (arranged in a vertical arc toward the middle of the flag) in the upper hoist-side corner the flag of Australia is used; note—in early 1986, the Christmas Island Assembly held a design competition for an island flag, however, the winning design has never been formally adopted as the official flag of the territory the flag of France is used the flag of Australia is used three horizontal bands of yellow (top, double-width), blue, and red; similar to the flag of Ecuador, which is longer and bears the Ecuadorian coat of arms superimposed in the center four equal horizontal bands of yellow (top), white, red, and blue with a green isosceles triangle based on the hoist; centered within the triangle is a white crescent with the convex side facing the hoist and four white, five-pointed stars placed vertically in a line between the points of the crescent; the horizontal bands and the four stars represent the four main islands of the archipelago— Mwali, Njazidja, Nzwani, and Mayotte (a territorial collectivity of France, but claimed by Comoros); the crescent, stars, and color green are traditional symbols of Islam light blue with a large yellow five-pointed star in the center and a columnar arrangement of six small yellow five-pointed stars along the hoist side divided diagonally from the lower hoist side by a yellow band; the upper triangle (hoist side) is green and the lower triangle is red; uses the popular pan-African colors of Ethiopia blue, with the flag of the UK in the upper hoist-side quadrant and a large circle of 15 white five-pointed stars (one for every island) centered in the outer half of the flag the flag of Australia is used five horizontal bands of blue (top), white, red (double width), white, and blue, with the coat of arms in a white elliptical disk on the hoist side of the red band; above the coat of arms a light blue ribbon contains the words, AMERICA CENTRAL, and just below it near the top of the coat of arms is a white ribbon with the words, REPUBLICA COSTA RICA three equal vertical bands of orange (hoist side), white, and green; similar to the flag of Ireland, which is longer and has the colors reversed—green (hoist side), white, and orange; also similar to the flag of Italy, which is green (hoist side), white, and red; design was based on the flag of France red, white, and blue horizontal bands with Croatian coat of arms (red and white checkered) five equal horizontal bands of blue (top and bottom) alternating with white; a red equilateral triangle based on the hoist side bears a white, five-pointed star in the center; design influenced by the US flag white with a copper-colored silhouette of the island (the name Cyprus is derived from the Greek word for copper) above two green crossed olive branches in the center of the flag; the branches symbolize the hope for peace and reconciliation between the Greek and Turkish communities two equal horizontal bands of white (top) and red with a blue isosceles triangle based on the hoist side (identical to the flag of the former Czechoslovakia) red with a white cross that extends to the edges of the flag; the vertical part of the cross is shifted to the hoist side, and that design element of the Dannebrog (Danish flag) was subsequently adopted by the other Nordic countries of Finland, Iceland, Norway, and Sweden the flag of the UK is used two equal horizontal bands of light blue (top) and light green with a white isosceles triangle based on the hoist side bearing a red five-pointed star in the center green, with a centered cross of three equal bands—the vertical part is yellow (hoist side), black, and white and the horizontal part is yellow (top), black, and white; superimposed in the center of the cross is a red disk bearing a sisserou parrot encircled by 10 green, five-pointed stars edged in yellow; the 10 stars represent the 10 administrative divisions (parishes) a centered white cross that extends to the edges divides the flag into four rectangles—the top ones are blue (hoist side) and red, and the bottom ones are red (hoist side) and blue; a small coat of arms featuring a shield supported by an olive branch (left) and a palm branch (right) is at the center of the cross; above the shield a blue ribbon displays the motto, DIOS, PATRIA, LIBERTAD (God, Fatherland, Liberty), and below the shield, REPUBLICA DOMINICANA appears on a red ribbon red, with a black isosceles triangle (based on the hoist side) superimposed on a slightly longer yellow arrowhead that extends to the center of the flag; there is a white star in the center of the black triangle three horizontal bands of yellow (top, double width), blue, and red with the coat of arms superimposed at the center of the flag; similar to the flag of Colombia, which is shorter and does not bear a coat of arms three equal horizontal bands of red (top), white, and black; the national emblem (a gold Eagle of Saladin facing the hoist side with a shield superimposed on its chest above a scroll bearing the name of the country in Arabic) centered in the white band; design is based on the Arab Liberation flag and similar to the flag of Syria, which has two green stars, Iraq, which has three green stars (plus an Arabic inscription) in a horizontal line centered in the white band, and Yemen, which has a plain white band three equal horizontal bands of blue (top), white, and blue with the national coat of arms centered in the white band; the coat of arms features a round emblem encircled by the words REPUBLICA DE EL SALVADOR EN LA AMERICA CENTRAL; similar to the flag of Nicaragua, which has a different coat of arms centered in the white band—it features a triangle encircled by the words REPUBLICA DE NICARAGUA on top and AMERICA CENTRAL on the bottom; also similar to the flag of Honduras, which has five blue stars arranged in an X pattern centered in the white band three equal horizontal bands of green (top), white, and red with a blue isosceles triangle based on the hoist side and the coat of arms centered in the white band; the coat of arms has six yellow six-pointed stars (representing the mainland and five offshore islands) above a gray shield bearing a silk-cotton tree and below which is a scroll with the motto UNIDAD, PAZ, JUSTICIA (Unity, Peace, Justice) red isosceles triangle (based on the hoist side) dividing the flag into two right triangles; the upper triangle is green, the lower one is blue; a gold wreath encircling a gold olive branch is centered on the hoist side of the red triangle pre-1940 flag restored by Supreme Soviet in May 1990—three equal horizontal bands of blue (top), black, and white three equal horizontal bands of green (top), yellow, and red with a yellow pentagram and single yellow rays emanating from the angles between the points on a light blue disk centered on the three bands; Ethiopia is the oldest independent country in Africa, and the three main colors of her flag were so often adopted by other African countries upon independence that they became known as the pan-African colors the flag of France is used blue with the flag of the UK in the upper hoist-side quadrant and the Falkland Island coat of arms centered on the outer half of the flag; the coat of arms contains a white ram (sheep raising is the major economic activity) above the sailing ship Desire (whose crew discovered the islands) with a scroll at the bottom bearing the motto DESIRE THE RIGHT white with a red cross outlined in blue extending to the edges of the flag; the vertical part of the cross is shifted toward the hoist side in the style of the Dannebrog (Danish flag) light blue with the flag of the UK in the upper hoist-side quadrant and the Fijian shield centered on the outer half of the flag; the shield depicts a yellow lion above a white field quartered by the cross of Saint George featuring stalks of sugarcane, a palm tree, bananas, and a white dove three equal vertical bands of blue (hoist side), white, and red; known as the "Le drapeau tricolore" (French Tricolor), the origin of the flag dates to 1790 and the French Revolution; the design and/or colors are similar to a number of other flags, including those of Belgium, Chad, Ireland, Cote d'Ivoire, Luxembourg, and Netherlands; the official flag for all French dependent areas the flag of France is used two narrow red horizontal bands encase a wide white band; centered on the white band is a disk with blue and white wave pattern on the lower half and gold and white ray pattern on the upper half; a stylized red, blue and white ship rides on the wave pattern; the French flag is used for official occasions the flag of France is used three equal horizontal bands of green (top), yellow, and blue three equal horizontal bands of red (top), blue with white edges, and green white rectangle, in its central portion a red cross connecting all four sides of the flag; in each of the four corners is a small red bolnur-katskhuri cross; the five-cross flag appears to date back to the 14th century three equal horizontal bands of black (top), red, and gold three equal horizontal bands of red (top), yellow, and green with a large black five-pointed star centered in the yellow band; uses the popular pan-African colors of Ethiopia; similar to the flag of Bolivia, which has a coat of arms centered in the yellow band two horizontal bands of white (top, double width) and red with a three-towered red castle in the center of the white band; hanging from the castle gate is a gold key centered in the red band the flag of France is used nine equal horizontal stripes of blue alternating with white; there is a blue square in the upper hoist-side corner bearing a white cross; the cross symbolizes Greek Orthodoxy, the established religion of the country two equal horizontal bands of white (top) and red with a large disk slightly to the hoist side of center—the top half of the disk is red, the bottom half is white a rectangle divided diagonally into yellow triangles (top and bottom) and green triangles (hoist side and outer side), with a red border around the flag; there are seven yellow, five-pointed stars with three centered in the top red border, three centered in the bottom red border, and one on a red disk superimposed at the center of the flag; there is also a symbolic nutmeg pod on the hoist-side triangle (Grenada is the world's second-largest producer of nutmeg, after Indonesia); the seven stars represent the seven administrative divisions the flag of France is used territorial flag is dark blue with a narrow red border on all four sides; centered is a red-bordered, pointed, vertical ellipse containing a beach scene, outrigger canoe with sail, and a palm tree with the word GUAM superimposed in bold red letters; US flag is the national flag three equal vertical bands of light blue (hoist side), white, and light blue with the coat of arms centered in the white band; the coat of arms includes a green and red quetzal (the national bird) and a scroll bearing the inscription LIBERTAD 15 DE SEPTIEMBRE DE 1821 (the original date of independence from Spain) all superimposed on a pair of crossed rifles and a pair of crossed swords and framed by a wreath white with the red cross of Saint George (patron saint of England) extending to the edges of the flag and a yellow equal-armed cross of William the Conqueror superimposed on the Saint George cross three equal vertical bands of red (hoist side), yellow, and green; uses the popular pan-African colors of Ethiopia two equal horizontal bands of yellow (top) and green with a vertical red band on the hoist side; there is a black five-pointed star centered in the red band; uses the popular pan-African colors of Ethiopia green, with a red isosceles triangle (based on the hoist side) superimposed on a long, yellow arrowhead; there is a narrow, black border between the red and yellow, and a narrow, white border between the yellow and the green two equal horizontal bands of blue (top) and red with a centered white rectangle bearing the coat of arms, which contains a palm tree flanked by flags and two cannons above a scroll bearing the motto L'UNION FAIT LA FORCE (Union Makes Strength) the flag of Australia is used two vertical bands of yellow (hoist side) and white with the crossed keys of Saint Peter and the papal miter centered in the white band three equal horizontal bands of blue (top), white, and blue with five blue, five-pointed stars arranged in an X pattern centered in the white band; the stars represent the members of the former Federal Republic of Central America—Costa Rica, El Salvador, Guatemala, Honduras, and Nicaragua; similar to the flag of El Salvador, which features a round emblem encircled by the words REPUBLICA DE EL SALVADOR EN LA AMERICA CENTRAL centered in the white band; also similar to the flag of Nicaragua, which features a triangle encircled by the word REPUBLICA DE NICARAGUA on top and AMERICA CENTRAL on the bottom, centered in the white band red with a stylized, white, five-petal bauhinia flower in the center the flag of the US is used three equal horizontal bands of saffron (subdued orange) (top), white, and green with a blue chakra (24-spoked wheel) centered in the white band; similar to the flag of Niger, which has a small orange disk centered in the white band two equal horizontal bands of red (top) and white; similar to the flag of Monaco, which is shorter; also similar to the flag of Poland, which is white (top) and red three equal horizontal bands of green (top), white, and red; the national emblem (a stylized representation of the word Allah in the shape of a tulip, a symbol of martyrdom) in red is centered in the white band; ALLAH AKBAR (God is Great) in white Arabic script is repeated 11 times along the bottom edge of the green band and 11 times along the top edge of the red band three equal horizontal bands of red (top), white, and black with three green five-pointed stars in a horizontal line centered in the white band; the phrase ALLAH AKBAR (God is Great) in green Arabic script—Allah to the right of the middle star and Akbar to the left of the middle star—was added in January 1991 during the Persian Gulf crisis; similar to the flag of Syria, which has two stars but no script, Yemen, which has a plain white band, and that of Egypt which has a gold Eagle of Saladin centered in the white band; design is based upon the Arab Liberation colors three equal vertical bands of green (hoist side), white, and orange; similar to the flag of Cote d'Ivoire, which is shorter and has the colors reversed—orange (hoist side), white, and green; also similar to the flag of Italy, which is shorter and has colors of green (hoist side), white, and red white with a blue hexagram (six-pointed linear star) known as the Magen David (Shield of David) centered between two equal horizontal blue bands near the top and bottom edges of the flag three equal vertical bands of green (hoist side), white, and red; similar to the flag of Ireland, which is longer and is green (hoist side), white, and orange; also similar to the flag of the Cote d'Ivoire, which has the colors reversed—orange (hoist side), white, and green diagonal yellow cross divides the flag into four triangles—green (top and bottom) and black (hoist side and outer side) the flag of Norway is used white with a large red disk (representing the sun without rays) in the center the flag of the US is used white with a diagonal red cross extending to the corners of the flag; in the upper quadrant, surmounted by a yellow crown, a red shield with the three lions of England in yellow the flag of the US is used three equal horizontal bands of black (top), representing the Abbassid Caliphate, white, representing the Ummayyad Caliphate, and green, representing the Fatimid Caliphate; a red isosceles triangle on the hoist side, representing the Great Arab Revolt of 1916, and bearing a small white seven-pointed star symbolizing the seven verses of the opening Sura (Al-Fatiha) of the Holy Koran; the seven points on the star represent faith in One God, humanity, national spirit, humility, social justice, virtue, and aspirations; design is based on the Arab Revolt flag of World War I the flag of France is used sky blue background representing the endless sky and a gold sun with 32 rays soaring above a golden steppe eagle in the center; on the hoist side is a "national ornamentation" in gold three equal horizontal bands of black (top), red, and green; the red band is edged in white; a large warrior's shield covering crossed spears is superimposed at the center the flag of the US is used the upper half is red with a yellow frigate bird flying over a yellow rising sun, and the lower half is blue with three horizontal wavy white stripes to represent the ocean three horizontal bands of blue (top), red (triple width), and blue; the red band is edged in white; on the hoist side of the red band is a white disk with a red five-pointed star white with a red (top) and blue yin-yang symbol in the center; there is a different black trigram from the ancient I Ching (Book of Changes) in each corner of the white field three equal horizontal bands of green (top), white, and red with a black trapezoid based on the hoist side; design, which dates to 1961, based on the Arab revolt flag of World War I red field with a yellow sun in the center having 40 rays representing the 40 Kyrgyz tribes; on the obverse side the rays run counterclockwise, on the reverse, clockwise; in the center of the sun is a red ring crossed by two sets of three lines, a stylized representation of the roof of the traditional Kyrgyz yurt three horizontal bands of red (top), blue (double width), and red with a large white disk centered in the blue band three horizontal bands of maroon (top), white (half-width), and maroon three horizontal bands of red (top), white (double width), and red with a green cedar tree centered in the white band divided diagonally from the lower hoist side corner; the upper half is white, bearing the brown silhouette of a large shield with crossed spear and club; the lower half is a diagonal blue band with a green triangle in the corner 11 equal horizontal stripes of red (top and bottom) alternating with white; there is a white five-pointed star on a blue square in the upper hoist-side corner; the design was based on the US flag plain green; green is the traditional color of Islam (the state religion) two equal horizontal bands of blue (top) and red with a gold crown on the hoist side of the blue band three equal horizontal bands of yellow (top), green, and red three equal horizontal bands of red (top), white, and light blue; similar to the flag of the Netherlands, which uses a darker blue and is shorter; design was based on the flag of France light green with a lotus flower above a stylized bridge and water in white, beneath an arc of five gold, five-pointed stars: one large in center of arc and four smaller a yellow sun with eight broadening rays extending to the edges of the red field two equal horizontal bands of red (top) and green with a vertical white band of the same width on hoist side three equal horizontal bands of black (top), red, and green with a radiant, rising, red sun centered in the black band 14 equal horizontal stripes of red (top) alternating with white (bottom); there is a blue rectangle in the upper hoist-side corner bearing a yellow crescent and a yellow 14-pointed star; the crescent and the star are traditional symbols of Islam; the design was based on the flag of the US red with a large green rectangle in the center bearing a vertical white crescent; the closed side of the crescent is on the hoist side of the flag three equal vertical bands of green (hoist side), yellow, and red; uses the popular pan-African colors of Ethiopia two equal vertical bands of white (hoist side) and red; in the upper hoist-side corner is a representation of the George Cross, edged in red red with the Three Legs of Man emblem (Trinacria), in the center; the three legs are joined at the thigh and bent at the knee; in order to have the toes pointing clockwise on both sides of the flag, a two-sided emblem is used blue with two stripes radiating from the lower hoist-side corner—orange (top) and white; there is a white star with four large rays and 20 small rays on the hoist side above the two stripes a light blue background is divided into four quadrants by a white cross; in the center of each rectangle is a white snake; the flag of France is used for official occasions green with a yellow five-pointed star above a yellow, horizontal crescent; the closed side of the crescent is down; the crescent, star, and color green are traditional symbols of Islam four equal horizontal bands of red (top), blue, yellow, and green the flag of France is used three equal vertical bands of green (hoist side), white, and red; the coat of arms (an eagle perched on a cactus with a snake in its beak) is centered in the white band light blue with four white five-pointed stars centered; the stars are arranged in a diamond pattern the flag of the US is used same color scheme as

Romania—three equal vertical bands of blue (hoist side), yellow, and red; emblem in center of flag is of a Roman eagle of gold outlined in black with a red beak and talons carrying a yellow cross in its beak and a green olive branch in its right talons and a yellow scepter in its left talons; on its breast is a shield divided horizontally red over blue with a stylized ox head, star, rose, and crescent all in black-outlined yellow two equal horizontal bands of red (top) and white; similar to the flag of Indonesia which is longer and the flag of Poland which is white (top) and red three equal, vertical bands of red (hoist side), blue, and red; centered on the hoist-side red band in yellow is the national emblem ("soyombo"—a columnar arrangement of abstract and geometric representation for fire, sun, moon, earth, water, and the yin-yang symbol) blue, with the flag of the UK in the upper hoist-side quadrant and the Montserratian coat of arms centered in the outer half of the flag; the coat of arms features a woman standing beside a yellow harp with her arm around a black cross red with a green pentacle (five-pointed, linear star) known as Sulayman's (Solomon's) seal in the center of the flag; red and green are traditional colors in Arab flags, although the use of red is more commonly associated with the Arab states of the Persian gulf; design dates to 1912 three equal horizontal bands of green (top), black, and yellow with a red isosceles triangle based on the hoist side; the black band is edged in white; centered in the triangle is a yellow five-pointed star bearing a crossed rifle and hoe in black superimposed on an open white book a large blue triangle with a yellow sunburst fills the upper left section and an equal green triangle (solid) fills the lower right section; the triangles are separated by a red stripe that is contrasted by two narrow white-edge borders blue with a narrow, horizontal, yellow stripe across the center and a large white 12-pointed star below the stripe on the hoist side; the star indicates the country's location in relation to the Equator (the yellow stripe) and the 12 points symbolize the 12 original tribes of Nauru the flag of the US is used red with a blue border around the unique shape of two overlapping right triangles; the smaller, upper triangle bears a white stylized moon and the larger, lower triangle bears a white 12-pointed sun three equal horizontal bands of red (top), white, and blue;

similar to the flag of Luxembourg, which uses a lighter blue and is longer; one of the oldest flags in constant use, originating with William I, Prince of Orange, in the latter half of the 16th century white, with a horizontal blue stripe in the center superimposed on a vertical red band, also centered; five white, five-pointed stars are arranged in an oval pattern in the center of the blue band; the five stars represent the five main islands of Bonaire, Curacao, Saba, Sint Eustatius, and Sint Maarten the flag of France is used blue with the flag of the UK in the upper hoist-side quadrant with four red five-pointed stars edged in white centered in the outer half of the flag; the stars represent the Southern Cross constellation three equal horizontal bands of blue (top), white, and blue with the national coat of arms centered in the white band; the coat of arms features a triangle encircled by the words REPUBLICA DE NICARAGUA on the top and AMERICA CENTRAL on the bottom; similar to the flag of El Salvador, which features a round emblem encircled by the words REPUBLICA DE EL SALVADOR EN LA AMERICA CENTRAL centered in the white band; also similar to the flag of Honduras, which has five blue stars arranged in an X pattern centered in the white band three equal horizontal bands of orange (top), white, and green with a small orange disk (representing the sun) centered in the white band; similar to the flag of India, which has a blue spoked wheel centered in the white band three equal vertical bands of green (hoist side), white, and green yellow with the flag of the UK in the upper hoist-side quadrant; the flag of the UK bears five yellow five-pointed stars—a large one on a blue disk in the center and a smaller one on each arm of the bold red cross three vertical bands of green (hoist side), white, and green with a large green Norfolk Island pine tree centered in the slightly wider white band blue, with a white, five-pointed star superimposed on the gray silhouette of a latte stone (a traditional foundation stone used in building) in the center, surrounded by a wreath red with a blue cross outlined in white that extends to the edges of the flag; the vertical part of the cross is shifted to the hoist side in the style of the Dannebrog (Danish flag) three horizontal bands of white, red, and green of equal width with a broad, vertical, red band on the hoist side; the national emblem (a khanjar dagger in its sheath superimposed on two crossed swords in scabbards) in white is centered near the top of the vertical band green with a vertical white band (symbolizing the role of religious minorities) on the hoist side; a large white crescent and star are centered in the green field; the crescent, star, and color green are traditional symbols of Islam light blue with a large yellow disk (representing the moon) shifted slightly to the hoist side the flag of the US is used divided into four, equal rectangles; the top quadrants are white (hoist side) with a blue five-pointed star in the center and plain red; the bottom quadrants are plain blue (hoist side) and white with a red five-pointed star in the center divided diagonally from upper hoist-side corner; the upper triangle is red with a soaring yellow bird of paradise centered; the lower triangle is black with five, white, five-pointed stars of the Southern Cross constellation centered three equal, horizontal bands of red (top), white, and blue with an emblem centered in the white band; unusual flag in that the emblem is different on each side; the obverse (hoist side at the left) bears the national coat of arms (a yellow five-pointed star within a green wreath capped by the words REPUBLICA DEL PARAGUAY, all within two circles); the reverse (hoist side at the right) bears the seal of the treasury (a yellow lion below a red Cap of Liberty and the words Paz y Justicia (Peace and Justice) capped by the words REPUBLICA DEL PARAGUAY, all within two circles) three equal, vertical bands of red (hoist side), white, and red with the coat of arms centered in the white band; the coat of arms features a shield bearing a vicuna, cinchona tree (the source of quinine), and a yellow cornucopia spilling out gold coins, all framed by a green wreath two equal horizontal bands of blue (top) and red with a white equilateral triangle based on the hoist side; in the center of the triangle is a yellow sun with eight primary rays (each containing three individual rays) and in each corner of the triangle is a small yellow five-pointed star blue with the flag of the UK in the upper hoist-side quadrant and the Pitcairn Islander coat of arms centered on the outer half of the flag; the coat of arms is yellow, green, and light blue with a shield featuring a yellow anchor two equal horizontal bands of white (top) and red; similar to the flags of Indonesia and Monaco which are red (top) and white two vertical bands of green (hoist side, two-fifths) and red (three-fifths) with the Portuguese coat of arms centered on the dividing line five equal horizontal bands of red (top and bottom) alternating with white; a blue isosceles triangle based on the hoist side bears a large, white, five-pointed star in the center; design initially influenced by the US flag, but similar to the Cuban flag, with the colors of the bands and triangle reversed maroon with a broad white serrated band (nine white points) on the hoist side the flag of France is used three equal vertical bands of blue (hoist side), yellow, and red; the national coat of arms that used to be centered in the yellow band has been removed; now similar to the flag of Chad, also resembles the flags of Andorra and Moldova three equal horizontal bands of white (top), blue, and red three horizontal bands of sky blue (top, double width), yellow, and green, with a golden sun with 24 rays near the fly end of the blue band blue with the flag of the UK in the upper hoist-side quadrant and the Saint Helenian shield centered on the outer half of the flag; the shield features a rocky coastline and three-masted sailing ship divided diagonally from the lower hoist side by a broad black band bearing two white, five-pointed stars; the black band is edged in yellow; the upper triangle is green, the lower triangle is red blue, with a gold isosceles triangle below a black arrowhead; the upper edges of the arrowhead have a white border a yellow sailing ship facing the hoist side rides on a dark blue background with yellow wavy lines under the ship; on the hoist side, a vertical band is divided into three parts: the top part (called ikkurina) is red with a green diagonal cross extending to the corners overlaid by a white cross dividing the rectangle into four sections; the middle part has a white background with an ermine pattern; the third part has a red background with two stylized yellow lions outlined in black, one above the other; these three heraldic arms represent settlement by colonists from the Basque Country (top), Brittany, and Normandy; the flag of France is used for official occasions three vertical bands of blue (hoist side), gold (double width), and green; the gold band bears three green diamonds arranged in a V pattern red with a blue rectangle in the upper hoist-side quadrant bearing five white five-pointed stars representing the Southern Cross constellation two equal horizontal bands of white (top) and light blue with the national coat of arms superimposed in the center; the coat of arms has a shield (featuring three towers on three peaks) flanked by a wreath, below a crown and above a scroll bearing the word LIBERTAS (Liberty) three horizontal bands of green (top), yellow (double width), and green with two black five-pointed stars placed side by side in the center of the yellow band and a red isosceles triangle based on the hoist side; uses the popular pan-African colors of Ethiopia green, a traditional color in Islamic flags, with the Shahada or Muslim creed in large white Arabic script (translated as "There is no god but God; Muhammad is the Messenger of God") above a white horizontal saber (the tip points to the hoist side); design dates to the early twentieth century and is closely associated with the Al Saud family which established the kingdom in 1932 three equal vertical bands of green (hoist side), yellow, and red with a small green five-pointed star centered in the yellow band; uses the popular pan-African colors of Ethiopia three equal horizontal bands of blue (top), white, and red five oblique bands of blue (hoist side), yellow, red, white, and green (bottom) radiating from the bottom of the hoist side three equal horizontal bands of light green (top), white, and light blue two equal horizontal bands of red (top) and white; near the hoist side of the red band, there is a vertical, white crescent (closed portion is toward the hoist side) partially enclosing five white five-pointed stars arranged in a circle three equal horizontal bands of white (top), blue, and red superimposed with the Slovak cross in a shield centered on the hoist side; the cross is white centered on a background of red and blue three equal horizontal bands of white (top), blue, and red, with the Slovenian seal (a shield with the image of Triglav, Slovenia's highest peak, in white against a blue background at the center; beneath it are two wavy blue lines depicting seas and rivers, and above it are three six-pointed stars arranged in an inverted triangle, which are taken from the coat of arms of the Counts of Celje, the great Slovene dynastic house of the late 14th and early 15th centuries); the seal is located in the upper hoist side of the flag centered in the white and blue bands divided diagonally by a thin yellow stripe from the lower hoist-side corner; the upper triangle (hoist side) is blue with five white five-pointed stars arranged in an X pattern; the lower triangle is green light blue with a large white five-pointed star in the center; blue field influenced by the flag of the UN two equal width horizontal bands of red (top) and blue separated by a central green band which splits into a horizontal Y, the arms of which end at the corners of the hoist side; the Y embraces a black isosceles triangle from which the arms are separated by narrow yellow bands; the red and blue bands are separated from the green band and its arms by narrow white stripes blue, with the flag of the UK in the upper hoist-side quadrant and the South Georgia and the South Sandwich Islands coat of arms centered on the outer half of the flag; the coat of arms features a shield with a golden lion centered; the shield is supported by a fur seal on the left and a penguin on the right; a reindeer appears above the shield, and below it on a scroll is the motto LEO TERRAM PROPRIAM PROTEGAT (Let the Lion Protect its Own Land) three horizontal bands of red (top), yellow (double width), and red with the national coat of arms on the hoist side of the yellow band; the coat of arms includes the royal seal framed by the Pillars of Hercules, which are the two promontories (Gibraltar and Ceuta) on either side of the eastern end of the Strait of Gibraltar yellow with two panels; the smaller hoist-side panel has two equal vertical bands of green (hoist side) and orange; the other panel is a large dark red rectangle with a yellow lion holding a sword, and there is a yellow bo leaf in each corner; the yellow field appears as a border around the entire flag and extends between the two panels three equal horizontal bands of red (top), white, and black with a green isosceles triangle based on the hoist side five horizontal bands of green (top, double width), white, red (quadruple width), white, and green (double width); there is a large, yellow, five-pointed star centered in the red band the flag of Norway is used three horizontal bands of blue (top), red (triple width), and blue; the red band is edged in yellow; centered in the red band is a large black and white shield covering two spears and a staff decorated with feather tassels, all placed horizontally blue with a golden yellow cross extending to the edges of the flag; the vertical part of the cross is shifted to the hoist side in the style of the Dannebrog (Danish flag) red square with a bold, equilateral white cross in the center that does not extend to the edges of the flag three equal horizontal bands of red (top), white, and black, colors associated with the Arab Liberation flag; two small green five-pointed stars in a horizontal line centered in the white band; former flag of the United Arab Republic where the two stars represented the constituent states of Syria and Egypt; similar to the flag of Yemen, which has a plain white band, Iraq, which has three green stars (plus an Arabic inscription) in a horizontal line centered in the white band, and that of Egypt, which has a gold Eagle of Saladin centered in the white band; the current design dates to 1980 three horizontal stripes of red (top), a wider stripe of white, and green; a gold crown surmounted by seven gold, five-pointed stars is located in the center of the white stripe divided diagonally by a yellow-edged black band from the lower hoist-side corner; the upper triangle (hoist side) is green and the lower triangle is blue five horizontal bands of red (top), white, blue (double width), white, and red five equal horizontal bands of green (top and bottom) alternating with yellow; there is a white five-pointed star on a red square in the upper hoist-side corner; uses the popular pan-African colors of Ethiopia the flag of New Zealand is used red with a bold red cross on a white rectangle in the upper hoist-side corner red with a white-edged black diagonal band from the upper hoist side to the lower fly side the flag of France is used red with a white disk in the center bearing a red crescent nearly encircling a red five-pointed star; the crescent and star are traditional symbols of Islam red with a vertical white crescent (the closed portion is toward the hoist side) and white five-pointed star centered just outside the crescent opening green field with a vertical red stripe near the hoist side, containing five carpet guls (designs used in producing rugs) stacked above two crossed olive branches similar to the olive branches on the UN flag; a white crescent moon and five white stars appear in the upper corner of the field just to the fly side of the red stripe blue, with the flag of the UK in the upper hoist-side quadrant and the colonial shield centered on the outer half of the flag; the shield is yellow and contains a conch shell, lobster, and cactus light blue with the flag of the UK in the upper hoist-side quadrant; the outer half of the flag represents a map of the country with nine yellow five-pointed stars symbolizing the nine islands six equal horizontal bands of black (top), yellow, red, black, yellow, and red; a white disk is superimposed at the center and depicts a red-crested crane (the national symbol) facing the hoist side two equal horizontal bands of azure (top) and golden yellow represent grainfields under a blue sky three equal horizontal bands of green (top), white, and black with a wider vertical red band on the hoist side blue field with the red cross of Saint George (patron saint of England) edged in white superimposed on the diagonal red cross of Saint Patrick (patron saint of Ireland), which is superimposed on the diagonal white cross of Saint Andrew (patron saint of Scotland); properly known as the Union Flag, but commonly called the Union Jack; the design and colors (especially the Blue Ensign) have been the basis for a number of other flags including other Commonwealth countries and their constituent states or provinces, as well as British overseas territories 13 equal horizontal stripes of red (top and bottom) alternating with white; there is a blue rectangle in the upper hoist-side corner bearing 50 small, white, five-pointed stars arranged in nine offset horizontal rows of six stars (top and bottom) alternating with rows of five stars; the 50 stars represent the 50 states, the 13 stripes represent the 13 original colonies; known as Old Glory; the design and colors have been the basis for a number of other flags, including Chile, Liberia, Malaysia, and Puerto Rico nine equal horizontal stripes of white (top and bottom) alternating with blue; there is a white square in the upper hoist-side corner with a yellow sun bearing a human face known as the Sun of May and 16 rays alternately triangular and wavy three equal horizontal bands of blue (top), white, and green separated by red fimbriations with a white crescent moon and 12 white stars in the upper hoist-side quadrant two equal horizontal bands of red (top) and green with a black isosceles triangle (based on the hoist side) all separated by a black-edged yellow stripe in the shape of a horizontal Y (the two points of the Y face the hoist side and enclose the triangle); centered in the triangle is a boar's tusk encircling two crossed namele leaves, all in yellow three equal horizontal bands of yellow (top), blue, and red with the coat of arms on the hoist side of the yellow band and an arc of seven white five-pointed stars centered in the blue band red with a large yellow five-pointed star in the center white, with a modified US coat of arms in the center between the large blue initials V and I; the coat of arms shows a yellow eagle holding an olive branch in one talon and three arrows in the other with a superimposed shield of vertical red and white stripes below a blue panel the flag of the US is used a large white modified Maltese cross—shifted a little off center toward the fly and slightly downward—on a red background; the flag of France outlined in white on two sides is in the upper hoist quadrant; the flag of France is used for official occasions three equal horizontal bands of red (top), white, and black; similar to the flag of Syria, which has two green stars and of Iraq which has three green stars (plus an Arabic inscription) in a horizontal line centered in the white band; also similar to the flag of Egypt, which has a heraldic eagle centered in the white band green with a panel of three vertical bands of red (hoist side), black, and orange below a soaring orange eagle, on the outer edge of the flag seven equal horizontal bands of green, yellow, red, black, red, yellow, and green with a white isosceles triangle edged in black with its base on the hoist side; a yellow Zimbabwe bird representing the long history of the country is superimposed on a red five-pointed star in the center of the triangle, which symbolizes peace; green symbolizes agriculture, yellow—mineral wealth, red—blood shed to achieve independence, and black stands for the native people red with a dark blue rectangle in the upper hoist-side corner bearing a white sun with 12 triangular rays on a blue field, 12 five-pointed gold stars arranged in a circle, representing the union of the peoples of Europe; the number of stars is fixed

Georgian Poems

I shall not speak of sun
or Georgia or treasures
but the treasures
of Georgian poetry's
peaks, forests, both
ancient and modern

Georgia is a land of poetry
Georgian forests and nature
and history and crystalline streams
have comb valleys, heard
by the sensitive ear
majestic forests, sun
their own struggle in them

millions of our country's
readers have a deep patriotism
now translated

deep gorges have a music
to breed poetic thought;
while the incessant found expression
ancient and modern in languages
has bred a sense of chivalry
in many a ballad and poem

the treasures of Georgian literature
now accessible to many

the published works of The Knight
in the Tiger's Skin
the word by word translation
of great epic poems
afford the English reader
pretending to be complete

an anthology including the
specimens of varied poetry
of the Georgian people from
the beginning of its majestic
development till to-day

I shall not speak of the
difficulties of translating exquisite
pain partly expressing original beauty

Georgia's Memory

To lack birds our chants caged
Loss-sound's forecast of fragment-air
Numerous soft wells suck music's
Lumber from our sills, harm on

East, and west: a sea, will come damp
Blanket pounded song, fields blossom
Tall-hours loom-hands weaved-land
Love soured as milk to cheese

A rocked hill cloister mumbles
Plums ripe with ant roads drop
Sit here with my lips' instrument
Our rivals too lax to wage now

Moist attack black adorned
Gently tuned my eyes yielding
My most melancholy maze
Constant clashes age my weeps to honey

Two Embrace

To aside our sharp hurls
Your name's breath like mine
Breeds of neighbors wading
Such parity-ignorant clergy

Yet the two of us sunflower, in
The still of finch's wing
All days into one like blind nest
Sun our just spreading

Pursues common over grief
The must to boil our musk between
Mountain shoulder river leaps
Two sides dulled: our embrace

Sad Feast

Wine is quit flame poor for
Ends steep my soles past stoned
Per happening to multiply my wound
These woe things about this world

Chanced tweed drowns in pangs of dye

A horn-filled life nectar punctures

Fancy plays—
        —Luck me a maid
Whose bosom accepts my expired line
On a wooled wind my shoulders fan
Reading mad water's cleavage

Will you fly where mortal men
Ream lead of true valor
Deed-mine our joy as duty

Death far there as emigrate
A nest under palms or hazelnut

Hugged one day by urn

Hopes floated into woe the ocean

The Eagle

Eagle-knot pride sears wounds
An ear glues to raven hair your eyes
Stored gulps of flame miscarry
To rising but fell frenzied history

Feast here now where the blood stain
Butcher-bosom crescent-loads
When winced we trade world with word
Slapped cheek by feather

Sure is the hill and pain below

The Too-late Two

Stirred love quakes my rib

From this our no new balm
Chain as prison now this sour plum
My wood's heat now warm wound
Sung toward home you that late

My eye waters as tree softs
The sea's salt air hazelnuts
Shells, my collected skin
Shelter too late, heart stung
I now hear stifles to my sorrow
Dove-staffed row to more woe
My bones' marrow inching
We now you there me this

Joy spilt strange taste
Hope jumps rabbit away
Chest weakens into flesh
Road coincides breasts no more

Your new address shakes my crib

Evening

"Are sons leap-beauty on the skies"
Hunch tears our eyes brings
The air soon fool telegraph
Bricked-castle fashioned present
Trembles in history on fault
Blood should turning gold
As sound us breath hold
Resin is country pruned
Swallow graduated to jackal
Expectant daughters' oxen wigs
Horizon becoming fired line
Two of us look at and blind
Soil and cloud to smoke
Ghost-cast building-net
My and your dying park, a
Rest purple shade thin dark

Georgia Still Is Sleeping

What canary climbs sand-oceans
Or scarred scrapes of sky-night
Coma braised in orgies by sun
Also gently sunk owned drink

Flaunting right sick by medals
Watt can air climate, this din ore

I want it to contribute to you
Want tenders peaks of dead salt
In a cloud or hinged try
Absent as God's yeasting
Shed upon our farm's firm highs
Goats all that formers glory
Every antique sweat's flow
Pouring ebony mites over belly
A seamed bowl shying forth, whispering
"Georgia still is sleeping"

For it weighs the down of light

Some Jockeying

Syria has been. Syria's history dates back to ancient empires. Syria maintains either a hot war or an uneasy ceasefire. Syria lost the Golan Heights. A number of conquerors.

Islam came to the region. For a period of time, the Ba'ath control. Damascus was the center of Islamic rule. The Turks arrived late. Crusaders over Lebanon. Saladin defeated Turks and Crusaders. The League of Nations. The Mamluk empire follows and Syria is twice attacked. Unhealthy stress Damascus. The Mamluk era. The Mamluks were professing loyalty to the sixteenth century. Ottomans cut. Turks retain control. Affairs include terrorism. The League of Nations placed a situation. Syria and Lebanon under France. French in Syria profess loyalty. The Vichy government. Britain together with Free French forces. Invasion of Syria. The creation of a Syrian republic. Hafez el-Assad. Complete independence. Syria has [been] an implacable foe. Through various configurations Damascus was the center. Syria has spent. An uneasy league. Tensions have persisted. Israel and Syria. Syria over Lebanon. The extremist Ba'ath. Syria has maintained a radical situation on Eastern affairs including the West. Syria's long-time leader Hafez el-Assad. This stance will doubt signification. The Turks arrived. The League of Nations placed. French forces invaded. The Mamluk empire followed.

Complete independence was declared. The twelfth century's Saladin succeeded. Tensions have persisted. In nineteen sixty seven, Syria lost. Syria professed loyalty. The Mongols. The Mamluk era. Ottomans. Party came. Conqueror controlled. Syria tried and failed. An uneasy ceasefire. Syria over Lebanon. In Israeli hands. Number of conquerors. Of Islamic rule. For fifty-plus years. Through various configurations.

Hands through Syria. Syria maintains. The extremist Ba'ath. Hafez el-Assad. Empire followed. Stance on most. History dates.

ARMS AND ARMS THROUGH

HISTORY'S SILVER EYES ERASE LIES. SYRIA
BECOMES CHARTER MEMBER OF UNITED
NATIONS. IT'S ONE THOUSAND NINE HUNDRED
FORTY SIX AD & BRITISH TROOPS LEAVE SYRIA.
SYRIA'S LONG, LONG HISTORY IS SYRIAN. IT'S
ONE THOUSAND NINE HUNDRED FORTY THREE
AD & THE NEW GOVERNMENT IN SYRIA IS
SYRIAN. IT'S ONE THOUSAND NINE HUNDRED
FORTY ONE AD & FREE FRENCH GOVERNMENT
RECOGNIZES SYRIA'S INDEPENDENCE. IT'S ONE
THOUSAND NINE HUNDRED FORTY ONE AD &
BRITISH AND FRENCH FORCES SUBDUE SYRIA.
IT'S ONE THOUSAND NINE HUNDRED FORTY AD
& VICHY GOVERNMENT CONTROLS SYRIA. IT'S
ONE THOUSAND NINE HUNDRED FORTY AD &
FRANCE FALLS. SYRIA SIDES WITH FRANCE AND
ALLIES. WORLD WAR TWO BEGINS. SYRIANS'
HOSTILITY IS RAISED TO NEW PITCH. IT'S ONE
THOUSAND NINE HUNDRED THIRTY NINE AD &
FRANCE CEDES ANCIENT ANTIOCH TO TURKEY.
IT'S ONE THOUSAND NINE HUNDRED THIRTY
EIGHT AD & FRANCE REFUSES TO RATIFY SYRIAN
INDEPENDENCE TREATY. IT'S ONE THOUSAND
NINE HUNDRED TWENTY & ONE THOUSAND
NINE HUNDRED TWENTY FIVE THROUGH
ONE THOUSAND NINE HUNDRED TWENTY
SEVEN AD & THE FRENCH MOVE TO QUELL
ARMED REBELLIONS. SYRIA'S NATIONALISM
IS MORE DETERMINED & SHIFTS FROM ANTI-
TURKISH TO ANTI-FRENCH SENTIMENT. IT'S
ONE THOUSAND NINE HUNDRED TWENTY AD
& FRANCE IS GRANTED MANDATE OVER SYRIA
AND LEBANON BY THE LEAGUE OF NATIONS. ALL
OF TIME IS PRESENT.

WESTERN WORDS NO LONGER CARRY HONOR FOR PATRIARCHS IN THE ARAB DESERTS. HISTORY DOCUMENTS COUNTLESS LIES AND DECEITS. GREAT BRITAIN AND FRANCE SECRETLY DECIDE THAT SYRIA AND MOST ARAB LANDS WILL BE DIVIDED INTO BRITISH AND FRENCH SPHERES. ALLIES PROMISE SYRIANS INDEPENDENCE IF THEY REBEL AGAINST TURKEY. TURKEY SIDES WITH CENTRAL POWERS. OTTOMAN EMPIRE BECOMES TURKEY THROUGH GENOCIDE. THE FIRST WORLD WAR BEGINS & SYRIAN NATIONALIST MOVEMENTS HOLD PARTS OF OTTOMAN EMPIRE. IT'S ONE THOUSAND NINE HUNDRED FOURTEEN THROUGH ONE THOUSAND NINE HUNDRED EIGHTEEN AD. IT'S ONE THOUSAND EIGHT HUNDRED SIXTY NINE AD & SYRIA'S COMMERCIAL IMPORTANCE IS DIMINISHED WITH THE OPENING OF THE SUEZ CANAL. OTTOMANS GRIP SYRIA FOR FOUR CENTURIES. IT'S ONE THOUSAND FIVE HUNDRED SIXTEEN AD & THE TURKS INCORPORATE SYRIA AND SURROUNDING REGIONS. SYRIA IS ABLE TO SEE HISTORY AT ONCE AND COMPLETELY.

IT'S ONE THOUSAND TWO HUNDRED SIXTY AD & SYRIA'S RUIN IS MADE COMPLETE BY A MONGOL INVASION. MANY WARS IMPOVERISH SYRIA'S LAND AND PEOPLE. IT'S ONE THOUSAND ONE HUNDRED EIGHTY SEVEN AD & SALADIN OVERTHROWS THE CROSS. IT'S ONE THOUSAND ONE HUNDRED SEVENTY FOUR THROUGH ONE THOUSAND ONE HUNDRED EIGHTY SEVEN AD & SALADIN TAKES SYRIA. IT'S ONE THOUSAND NINETY NINE AD & CRUSADERS INCORPORATE SYRIA AND SURROUNDING REGIONS INTO CHRISTIAN KINGDOM. IRAQ IS A NEWER SPLENDID MUSLIM WORLD. DAMASCUS IS SUPPLANTED BY BAGHDAD IN IRAQ. THERE ARE NOBLE PATRIARCHS IN THE DESERTS OF SYRIA. IT IS A MOST IMPORTANT AND SPLENDID MUSLIM WORLD. THE CALIPH'S EYES GRAZE HISTORY WITH GREAT CHARM, HARMONY, AND ELEGANCE. IT'S SIX HUNDRED SIXTY ONE AD & DAMASCUS IS THE SEAT OF POWERFUL CALIPHS. A JOURNEY THROUGH SYRIA IS A JOURNEY THROUGH TIME. IT'S SIX HUNDRED THIRTY SIX AD & SYRIA'S ARABS ARE ABSORBED BY EXPANDING ISLAMIC EMPIRE. SYRIA IS BYZANTINE FOR TWENTY ONE THOUSAND SEVEN HUNDRED DAYS. CONSTANTINOPLE IS NOW CAPITAL. SYRIA'S KINGDOM IS CONQUERED BY EGYPT, BABYLON, WESTERN ROMAN EMPIRE, AND BYZANTINE EMPIRE. SYRIA'S FAR-FLUNG DOMINIONS ARE DIVIDED INTO TWO PARTS. SYRIA IS A LONG HISTORY.

HISTORY IN SYRIA IS SOMETHING THAT LIVES. IT'S SOON THEREAFTER & SYRIA IS GRANTED INDEPENDENCE. IT'S SIX HUNDRED THIRTY SIX AD & IT'S CONQUERED BY ARABS AND ABSORBED INTO EXPANDING ARAB EMPIRE. IT'S SIXTY FOUR BC & SYRIA IS ROMAN. SYRIA LOOKS AT HISTORY & IT TELLS TRUTHS. SYRIA'S EYES ARE SILVER. AREAS OF WESTERN ASIA BECOME SYRIA. IT'S THIRD CENTURY BC & PTOLOMIES OF EGYPT & SELEUCIDS CONTEND FOR LOWER SYRIA & PALESTINE. IT'S THREE HUNDRED THIRTY TWO BC & ALEXANDER'S GENERAL FOUNDS ANTIOCH AS CAPITAL. IT'S THREE HUNDRED THIRTY THREE BC & ALEXANDER'S EMPIRE SACKS SYRIA. IT'S FIFTH CENTURY BC & REGION IS TAKEN BY PERSIANS. IT'S SIXTH CENTURY BC & REGION PASSES TO THE CHALDEANS. IT'S EIGHTH CENTURY BC & PARTS OF SYRIA ARE TAKEN BY ASSYRIA. IT'S EIGHTH CENTURY BC & PARTS OF SYRIA ARE CONQUERED BY EGYPTIANS AND HITTITES. IT'S ONE THOUSAND EIGHT HUNDRED BC & SYRIA IS RECORDED. IT IS TIME WHICH IN SYRIA IS ALWAYS PRESENT. HISTORY IN SYRIA IS SOMETHING LIVING.

Worth Remember

Syria is beautiful

Syria's long
long history

Syria has monuments

In 1967
Syria lost

Syria professed loyalty

Syria over Lebanon

Syria has
Maintained

Hands through Syria

Syria was recorded

Syria Is in the World

Every person has two homelands. Syria is the cradle of civilizations. Civilizations emerged as the product of Syria's indigenous people. Others (civilizations) came from abroad establishing contexts of exchange, reaching the most fertile interaction known to humanity. Thousands of archeological sites attest that history is condensed in Syria, the greatest small country in the world. Syrian people are friendly and peaceful.

All possible individual personalities in human beings hold in possession one more than one areas set aside to be a state for a people of a particular national, cultural, or racial origin.

Syria is the most beautiful destination in the world. Syria made copper pliable. Syria's long, long history invented bronze. Syria's glory is not only in the present. If you are interested in history then Syria is the most under-advertised important country in the world. Any visitor to Syria (where crime rate is low) will say the same thing. Syria is one of the most beautiful destinations. Syrian people are peaceful. Syrians were first to wear hand-weaved cotton and silk cloths. This is why (rightfully) Syria was called the cradle of civilizations. Modern man is indebted.

The Silk Road caravans were not only for carrying goods.

Nature in Syria is very diverse. We are adding new pictures, ranging from forests in the north-west (where there are an abundance of palaces) to beaches on Syria's Mediterranean coast (where there are an abundance of palaces) and Syria's bread baskets in the north-east and the south (where there are an abundance of palaces).

Syria's streets are among the world's safest; the crime rate is very low and people wander the streets in Syria's nights. Syrian people are friendly.

If you are interested in history and historical monuments, you cannot miss Syria; there is a monument around every corner; there is no civilization in the east or west (throughout world history) that didn't pass through Syria and leave a mark in Syria as well as being effected by Syria, Syria's long, long history. A cradle for civilizations.

Food in Syria is very tasty and famous. Syria is often the largest small country in the world. Syria has a long, long history. The Bronze civilization came. (Ten thousand years ago) agriculture began. Houses, not caves, became man's dwellings.

All possible individual personalities in human beings hold in possession one more than one areas set aside to be a state for a people of a particular national, cultural, or racial origin.

Syria is one of the destinations in the world. Today we still admire fabric. Syria is the cradle of the great civilization; the accomplishments of her ancients are renowned. Syrian people are friendly and peaceful. The Islamic conquest only confirmed Syria's Arab identity (gave a tense to the land).

It was in Syria that soil was tamed, settlement commenced, civilization emerged. Journey through Syria is journey through time. Silk Road caravans were for carrying goods. Houses became man's dwellings; man embarked on journey of self-discovery. He observed heaven and sang hymns; tried his hand at drawing and sculpture. These ancient arts are found all over Syria. You are interested in monuments.

Syria also produced the world with another discovery. Copper was made pliable and bronze invented. The Bronze civilization came. By the Euphrates and elsewhere, there was an abundance of palaces, temples and murals reflecting cultural and commercial activity. Syria is in the world. Syria's visit is worth visiting the world.

Human beings making up a group or linked by a common characteristic or interest native to or inhabiting Syria are not hostile but in a state of calm and quiet.

Syria is beautiful. Successive waves of migration make it beautiful, and if you are interested in monuments, you cannot miss Syria. The Arab Peninsula gave an Arab identity to Syria, and it managed to withstand invasions by Hittites, Persians, Greeks and Romans. The Islamic conquest gave a sense of the land, adding new pictures and additional information. Syria is now the most beautiful world.

Today we admire the fabric on Syrian women during happy events and occasions as a witness of the old cultural interaction embraced by a land called Syria whose visit is visiting the world.

Natives or inhabitants of Syria preceded all others in time in using as an article of clothing or adornment a soft fibrous usually white substance composed of hairs attached to the seeds of a plant related to the mallow and a fine strong lustrous protein fiber produced by insect larvae usually for their cocoons produced on hand-operated looms.

The strategic importance of Syria is due to her unique position as a meeting place of Asia, Africa, and Europe, and as a crossroad between the Caspian, the Indian, the Black, and the Nile waters. Through Syria (food in Syria is famous) lay the silk route which led from China to Doura Europos, from Palmyra and Homs to the Mediterranean, where for thousands of years Syrian seafarers had ridden the wave in their enormous fleets with gleaming white sails.

This geographical position lent distinction. Syria has a long, long history not only as a trade and caravan route, but also a weave of diverse ideas, beliefs, talents, and cultures. Syria absorbed heaven and sang the earliest hymns.

A journey through Syria (because it managed to withstand invasions) is a journey through time. Syrian people are friendly and peaceful. Syrian seafarers had ridden waves with gleaming white sails. Syrians offered man his alphabet.

Human beings native to Syria are not hostile but in a state of calm and quiet.

When you enter the old souks (murals reflect cultural and commercial activity) you realize that history is sometimes alive and tangible, something you can see and touch. You go down the street which stretches and you feel that you are walking beside Saul of Tarsus when he saw lights of faith; the lights lead to Damascus.

The silk weavers whom you see in Damascus, Hama and Aleppo still work at their wooden handlooms just like their ancestors did in fleets with gleaming white sails years ago. Glass blowers at their brick furnaces recall their predecessors who invented friendly and peaceful glass.

(We will tell you Syrian people are friendly and peaceful and you will hear about the added sections when we add them). Folk artists still draw pictures of epic seafarers and man's first alphabet (almost identical to those engraved on stone by artists in the years B. C.).

Syria's long, long history. Syria's lively summer nights. Syria's oft description as the largest small country in the world. Syria's wealth as an ancient civilization. Journey through Syria is journey through time. Modern man is much of Syria's thought and learning. It is aptly said that every person has two homelands: his own, Syria.

Every person's homeland: Syria, the cradle of civilizations. Some of these civilizations emerged as the product of its indigenous people while the others came from abroad establishing a unique context of exchange and reaching the most fertile interaction ever known to humanity. Thousands of archeological sites scattered all over Syria attest that history is condensed in Syria, described as the greatest small country in the world. Syria is friendly and peaceful.

For thousands of years, this unrivalled geographical position was the main attraction for many civilizations. A journey of caravans from four directions to all destinations met at this place, allowing the fusion of most refined cultures with Syria's famous food. Therefore, its people got the tradition of hospitality and warmth of the heart. Syrians gave sense to other lands.

In the shadow of the bazaars (by the Euphrates and elsewhere) Syrian people are friendly and peaceful. The khans, and men from everywhere, accompanied caravans communicating and creating where they were able to dialogue and to enjoy the hospitality of the inhabitants of the blessed land of Syria. A journey through Syria (the silk weavers whom you see in Damascus, Hama and Aleppo still work at their wooden handlooms just like their ancestors did in Ebla four thousand years ago) is a journey through time. When you enter the old souks you realize that history is time alive and tangible, moist clay, an alive alphabet.

The Amorites, the Kanaanites and Phoenicians inhabited the coastal regions, the Arameans were the highlanders, and the Nabateans inhabited the south. Syrian seafarers inhabited water with their enormous fleets with gleaming sails, enjoying Syria's lively summer nights from sea. Syrian skilled craftsmen changed the silk into wonderful poets, scholars, travelers, and musicians. Traders accompanied cloths that are to this day the most beautiful perfection in the art of textile. Syrians wore hand-weaved cotton and silk cloths. Veils worn by Palmyrean women, shown over the many statues, are made from those fabrics. History is tangible.

You have an interest in history. You cannot miss Syria. Syria has monuments. The Euphrates is elsewhere. Modern man is now learning. Syria's streets are worlds. Syrian people are. Finally, food in Syria is very tasty and famous.